YES YOU CAN!

YES YOU CAN!

*Commitment and Strategies
for Overcoming Bipolar
and Unipolar Depression*

by

Richard Aaron Mead

REGENT PRESS
2001

First Printing

Library of Congress Cataloging-in-Publication Data

Mead, Richard Aaron
  Yes you can! : commitment and strategies for overcoming bipolar and unipolar depression / by Richard Aaron Mead.
    p. cm.
  ISBN 1-58790-004-1
  1. Mead, Richard Aaron. 2. Manic-depressive illness--Patients--Biography. 3. Depression, Mental--Patients--Biography. 4. Affective disorders--Patients--Biography. I. Title.

RC516 .M42 2001
616.89'5'0092--dc21
  [B]   00-051748

Manufactured in the United States of America
Regent Press
6020A Adeline
Oakland, CA 94608

regent@sirius.com

Dedicated to my daughters, LILIA and DARYA and to their mother, CYNTHIA. Without their love and encouragement over many years, I would have had no chance, and no story to tell.

Acknowledgements

To my lifelong friends and icons at **MDDA** (Boston): Anne Whitman and Dennis Hagler, who were always there when I needed them. In distinctly different ways, their support and warmth pulled me back from the abyss.

To Wendy Woodfield and Henry Seider for their continuing friendship. To Margaret Lichtenberg for her long association and forbearance. To Betsey Biggs for her valued work in assembling the book.

And to Tom Herman, a special friend at **DMDA**, for his editorial insights, on-going work on promotion, and moral support.

Contents

Preface

Cynthia Nicholls Mead

This is such an important and necessary book. Richard and I were married for eighteen years —and now divorced for the same years. I can say in the present, and as I look back, that the time together and apart has been a journey as well as a process.

Unfortunately, when we were married we didn't have the benefit of good counseling or diagnostic tools and treatment. I think of bipolar as a condition rather than an illness or disease. Once Richard had diagnosis and treatment, he never ceased to work with it, or get the best therapy and treatment both medically and therapeutically. He also sought a well-recommended psychopharmacologist and always worked with the issues at hand.

In the midst of it all, he has stayed connected to me,

his family, friends, and most importantly, he has helped raise two wonderful daughters who embrace him. It has been so important to all of us to share in his progress and accomplishments. That he has written this book to help and inspire others is a tribute to his great ability to communicate and share

When events in people's lives can tear them apart and hope seems dim, it is a gift to seek out some words of wisdom and life experiences to give comfort, hope and reassurance along with concrete strategies. *Yes You Can!* is one of these gifts.

Foreword

Eric C. Dessain, M.D.

I n the summer of 1997, an esteemed friend and patient recommended me to Richard Mead, with whom I met regularly and continue to consult, despite his relocation to San Francisco. (He visits me in Boston three times a year).

Working with many disabled unipolar and bipolar clients allows me limited time for illusion. The facts about mental illness are sobering. This is why I enjoy seeing and hearing from Richard, whose demeanor belies a not atypical bipolar history (including an early hospitalization at Payne Whitney Clinic in New York). He brings a vision, candor and life force which people in my profession don't always see.

His insights and sensitivity to depression issues and to depressives are assets to the movement. His is an understanding borne of acute personal struggle, endurance, and ultimately triumph. But he shares with us mostly what experience has taught about triumph. In doing so, he reveals enthusiasm, humor, writing skills and, above all, determination to impact on his own life and the lives of others with mental illness.

The voice and message are new ones, adding to more traditional (and essential) professional approaches. We must take seriously the lessons the author has learned. They can open minds and options.

I don't think such a book has been written by one who has personally experienced, labored with (for fifteen years), and emerged intact from bipolar disorder with a vision sharing all that has worked for him. I salute this.

The author wastes almost no time in commiserating or reviewing details of his past. He focuses, rather, on suggesting practical things which others really can do for themselves.

This could be the clearest and most rewarding non-medical, 'non-professional' plea for health and well-being we have heard. Its simplicity disarms, delights and uplifts while it challenges!

Author's Note:

Dr. Eric C. Dessain is a highly regarded psychopharmacologist. A native Belgian, he received a B.S. and M.D. at Louvain University in Belgium. He was a Resident in Psychiatry at McLean Hospital outside Boston, Massachusetts, U.S.A. His academic appointments include Clinical Fellow, Research Fellow and Instructor in Psychiatry at Harvard Medical School. He is widely published and traveled, lecturing at national and international scientific meetings throughout the United States and Europe.

Dr. Dessain recently became a commissioned officer in the U.S. Army Medical Corps.

Background

Dennis H. Hagler

*Former President of MDDA Boston
and longtime friend*

I am honored to be a part of *Yes You Can!* I'm just one of the 11 million other reluctant experts in the growing population of people who suffer an affective illness—manic depression.

What is depression or manic depression? Some people believe it is a spiritual disease—a flight, then loss of spirit. Some think it must come from the past—something that was done to them, or something they did. Some see it as a chemical imbalance, a genetic roll of the dice. Or it must stem from weakness of will—"You don't need drugs... What you need is a job."

Most people, however, think of it as something they don't think about at all. It's okay on Oprah, but not next door, not in my department at work, and certainly not in my family. They just don't understand, nor do they want to.

Sometimes people need someone to feel better than, so they can feel better about themselves. The mentally ill fit this role nicely... "The mentally ill did it to themselves. Let them undo it themselves." As one-third of the homeless population, when you see one coming your way with Hefty-Bag suit and shopping cart, have you ever thought, "what loss, what misfortune, what change of luck, twist of fate, turn of health, could make me one of them?"

I certainly thought it could never be me. It was thirty years ago, 1970. I was a graduate engineer in the Peace Corps ready to change the world. Life was a joy, a challenge, an adventure. Then it happened. What remained was a vacuum, drawing me inward. Self-absorbed and disconnected my voice became shallow and shaky. I hated to hear myself talk. I had nothing to say.

Which brings me to the first night I attended the Manic Depressive and Depressive Association of Boston (MDDA-Boston). When I stepped into McLean Hospital that September night of 1989, I was stunned by a cacophony of voices and battered by a blur of unfamiliar faces. I could see I wasn't going to fit in. I knew I wasn't coming back.

Everyone there was so different, so ordinary. They came in every conceivable age, shape and attire. There were housewives and house husbands, successes and failures, reluctant heroes and ignored heroines. I found myself putting on a blue name tag and pretended to read pamphlets that were stacked along a table—the 'Welcoming Table.' Looking up, I saw a woman announcing the twelve Share/Care groups that would run simultaneously that evening: "Dealing with Depression, Mania, Young Adults, Women's Issues, Parenting, Friends and Family Room 132. Newcomers are in Room 117." That's where I went. I was a 'Newcomer.'

It wasn't till we started talking that I noticed that these people were like me. They were more like me than anyone I knew, and I realized that in here it was all right to let your guard down, to let the secret out. For the first time, when I talked about depression, I was understood completely, without judgment. For all our differences, the people in this room connected in a way I had not experienced before. Strangers shared their deepest fears and greatest triumphs, even if their greatest triumph was getting up, showering and getting there. We knew the heroic nature of that act.

The most difficult cross to bear with this disease is the inability to be understood by others who don't suffer from it. The horror of depression, the way we feel it, is beyond description. There is a comfort, however, in being understood and accepted. In MDDA, I found that understanding and acceptance.

People come every week to MDDA who are in the depths of depression. Sometimes they laugh. In that fleeting second, the miracle of MDDA becomes apparent — through helping others, we may save ourselves.

I am currently on the Board of Directors of MDDA-Boston. I was its president for two years and have facilitated over 500 groups. I've seen thousands of people with this disease and heard thousands of their stories. I remember most of them.

I remember a group eight years ago. A man came in, well dressed, well spoken but shattered, depressed, hesitant to trust and not quite ready to believe. This was Richard. He was on the edge of losing all he valued and thought defined him: job, career, relationship of twelve years, the affection of his daughters, the esteem of friends, peers and self. And this was only part of the unrelenting pain of depression.

As he came weekly to our self-help group, I noticed that although his losses grew, his strength started to return. One of the keys to this transformation was Prozac, one of many medications available for depression. Getting better is only a part of the process, however. Richard was getting well, a path that requires more than just medication.

His journey to well-being is long and personal and will continue throughout his life. This is a serious illness with a grim impact on the lives of too many people of all ages and backgrounds. It is universal, pervasive and hidden. Now, as an author, he has bravely decided to reveal his 'hidden passage' through manic depression. Knowing his personality, and having watched his transformation from victim to animated mentor, I am not entirely surprised.

The story that follows is not a self-indulgent, intro-spective confessional. This has been done before. It is rather an easy-to-read primer, a guide to freeing oneself from depression. What the author reveals is not scientif-ic.

He has carefully reevaluated and shared his life expe-riences, focusing on the years since 1993 when he most succeeded.

In our eight year association, Richard has traveled (mostly on his own) to China, Thailand, Hong Kong, Burma (Myanmar), Malaysia, Indonesia, Singapore, Vietnam, Taiwan, South Korea, Japan, Brazil, India, Nepal and Tibet. He moved from Boston to San Francisco where he remains engaged in support groups. He has seen one daughter marry and another give birth. He continues to acknowledge his own vulnerability, yet maintains creative standards as a writer, performing artist and world traveler.

His book is an original statement of love to all of us.

Dennis Hagler
Boston, Massachusetts

Introduction

"Life begins on the other side of despair."
– Jean-Paul Sartre

T he way to know something is to do it. The way to own something is to live it, to make it yours...

At a low point in my long battle with bipolar depression, in 1992, I told Dr. David MacMillan in Boston, "I will never surrender to the illness." I never did.

This was an affirmation which now, eight years later, leads me to write for those similarly afflicted, for their families and friends, and for all the disbelievers.

Hundreds of hours listening and talking with depressives and manic depressives have not desensitized me to their stories and their anguish. If I can help any of them—and I can—I don't write in vain.

Over fifteen years, once diagnosed (and perhaps the twenty-five prior to that), I encountered what the writer William Styron and the actress Patty Duke, among others, depicted graphically in their books.

Starting with a hospitalization at the Payne Whitney Clinic in New York in 1981, and followed by four and a half chaotic months unable to function or smile, I experienced much of the discord and disability known to the illness. This I will spare you.

Almost every effort I made until Memorial Day of 1994 was compromised and confused by 'it.' This included career, all relationships, stability, peace of mind, and organization. Planning ahead wasn't even on the agenda.

The quality of daily life was strained, as was the mechanism for solving problems. The weight of vulnerability was constant. Not the humanizing kind of vulnerability, but the weakening, self-defeating, confidence-eroding kind. In the late Spring of 1994, this changed...

Looking back many years, at age seventeen, at a very traditional and academic small eastern college, I fell apart shortly after arriving: I was suddenly lost and spinning harshly in a cycle of fright and uncertainty that made college life a nightmare. All the more so because those around me were busy finding themselves.

Nobody, least of all me, knew what was happening; and of course mental aberrations bore so grave a stigma that one hesitated to talk about it. The Dean, a comparatively humane figure, sent me to the head of the Psychology Department, who said something about my "not having cut the umbilical cord."

I was unable to study with any consistency and therefore surprised myself by finishing the year and later graduating without distinction or self-knowledge. Life was too often dominated by a fear of falling. This was a prologue to discomfort and panic, not growth.

Such was the isolation and ignorance of what we now call mental illness, in those days. Who knows the cost of this from that time until the diagnosis in 1981?

From 1981 to 1994 I was under treatment for Bipolar Disorder. There were good moments and bad; but even in remission, the illness colored my judgments and movements.

Early in 1994, a renowned New York psychopharmacologist prescribed an anti-depressant he had raved about for months. So much so that I was convinced it would work.

The 'gestation' period, eight weeks, seemed a lifetime. When the pill—which has done wonders for several friends—finally and dramatically failed me, I was crushed, as was my long-time girlfriend whose patience was already wearing thin.

Dr. MacMillan told me not to lose hope, saying "there are many other anti-depressants: I want to put you on Prozac immediately." At that time, I was also trying acupuncture and had just joined the TM (Transcendental Meditation) Movement in Cambridge, MA and started to meditate with some consistency.

Three days after starting Prozac, and perhaps a week

after starting to meditate, the depression lifted. With the help of those habits and strategies described in the pages that follow, it has not returned in the last six and a half years.

Understanding, achievement and confidence in my ability to cope, let alone to find personal joy and authentic selfhood, did not come quickly. Over six years, however, it has come with a clarity that nourishes, while extending a future I never thought could be mine.

Suspend your disbelief as you read. We must crawl before we can walk. This can be your experience if you are determined and patient.

Chapter 1
MDDA and DMDA

"We few, we happy few, we band of brothers;
For he today that sheds his blood with me
shall be my brother."
– William Shakespeare, Henry V

hese two branches (Boston and San Francisco) of the same Manic Depressive and Depressive Association were the sources for connecting with other depressives and manic depressives where I lived.

In 1981, in Manhattan, distressed and feeling helpless, I combed the medical community for a support organization or meeting. Had I found one, life would have been less isolated and more hopeful.

Isolation seems both the instinct and the destiny of the seriously depressed. Unfortunately, it is self-perpetuating and limiting and should be resisted. It does not serve past the lowest moments.

Isolation fosters isolation. In the Boston and San Francisco Associations, I found one antidote: men and women of all ages who, sharing the illness, could accept and exchange with others, however imperfectly. At the very least, this provided relief and refuge against a world that seemed unknowing and unfriendly to mental illness.

Chapter 2
Medication
&
Therapy

he two critical components and the least common denominators of depressive treatment are often misperceived. This is partly why many diagnosed as bipolar or unipolar avoid medication and fall short of commitment to therapy.

Financial hardship and inadequate medical insurance are also frequent realities. This is a tragedy of its own that I will leave to lawyers specializing in legislative matters for the disabled. Claudia Center of DMDA in San Francisco is the best source I know for this. Because of Claudia and other board leaders of DMDA and other associations nationally, mental illness is no longer a secret. Then again, the illness almost by definition erodes both critical thinking abilities and self-assurance. Little wonder that negotiating and generally protecting self-interest are impaired with medication. We mostly take what psychiatrists prescribe. This is still far from a science, though perhaps improving fast.

Few with our illness are able to take solace from the progress made by medical science in anti-depressant and related drugs. We cannot always see how far the industry has come. That is, unless we have benefited dramatically.

The two 'superstars' of depression, Lithium and Prozac, rescued me. The former in 1981, and the latter in 1994. I continue to take these two. Why tamper with success? Once dropped, the drugs will often not work again on the same person.

Prozac stabilized me in three days—an extraordinary response. As mentioned earlier, I had a disastrous run with another highly touted anti-depressant after high recommendations. This was a low point.

Keep trying, there are some great new meds out. This is one of the toughest issues. To endure side effects and then wait is a grueling exercise every time. But hang tough. A grim defeat led me to a liberating second try.

Above all, seek the services of a good psychopharmacologist. Once a month for a start and maybe once every other month if things work well. This is a psychiatrist who specializes in drugs.

My good friends Anne Whitman and Henry Seider, and my older daughter Darya, ganged up on me on a four-day boat odyssey on the Amazon in Brazil in 1996. Anne, as usual, led the assault. "You're overmedicated. I want you to see my doctor. You two will get along." The meeting was later arranged.

Dr. Eric Dessain in Boston patiently fine-tuned my medications, eliminated sluggishness, and recreated mental acuity. He was unconventional and unafraid. We were matched in heaven. I saw daylight.

Drug selection seems too arbitrary among DMDA members in San Francisco. Find a specialist and at least improve your chances. You needn't see one regularly. And then you have two professionals judging your meds.

Side Effects

Both those who use medication regularly and those who have rejected it are tormented by side effects. Sometimes these rival or surpass the symptoms they claim to eliminate. As many others, I originally forgot the warning about side effects and was overwhelmed when they showed up, often blaming psychiatrists for not giving good enough warnings.

Discuss this beforehand with your doctor. Factor in the side effects with your decision. Tell your doctor what you want to avoid. Later on, though it may be less desirable, bothersome side effects can be neutralized without reducing therapeutic benefits—try a change. Speak out. Take some control. A big step in the right direction. If you do nothing else, get this right. Resist the urge to give up all control. "A healthy organism protects itself." Start here. Make a difference.

The issue of what level of dosage you take is also

important. An expert not only decides this well for you but doesn't hesitate to alter his original decision for maximum therapeutic effect with minimal side effects. Too many don't look at their dosage and don't urge changes. This is often the way of things under severe symptoms or when hopes wane. But think about it.

Also, defer to the ideas of the doctor who sees you regularly. I made the mistake of acting on the suggestion of someone I saw every year or two. It cost two grim months on an anti-depressant that failed me.

Application of drugs is not yet a science in mental illness. Let's hope it will become one in the future. So do your best. Maximize your chance for success. Learn as much as you can about medications chosen for you. Listen to what you can learn from others. All of this keeps you 'engaged' with your treatment, as you should be.

It will come as no surprise to most readers that medications should be taken regularly and at close to the same time. There are problems among those who refuse medication for the wrong reason or take them irregularly. The rest of us aren't thrilled about depending on pills. We just take them.

I have felt better for more than six years. Yet I've taken Lithium for nineteen years and Prozac for six (though the level has been reduced three times). I will not play Russian roulette by stopping them now. There are too many stories of those who come off pills on their own because they feel a little better. But as I write this, my M.D./therapist is again urging that I reduce my daily Lithium intake. I'm always impressed by such resolve.

Therapy

Good therapy should be a combination of support and confrontation. Nobody will be surprised to hear that trust, honesty and commitment are critical to results: yet so many people fall short of these goals. They think that therapy "is applied to them, happens to them, is practiced on them."

We can work in therapy, we can challenge it, we can give it direction. Unfortunately, again, this may be easier when we feel better. On the other hand, we might take more risks when in crisis.

Tell your therapist when he or she has helped you with an observation. These are people, too; they may be reassured or inspired by your feedback. It will come back to you. Whenever someone complains that their therapist never says anything, I see red flags. Speak up.

Sometimes we show our therapist our best face, our animated look of the week. In Boston, mine didn't realize how depressed I was for months... because I was busy acting manic. Basically, I was thrilled to be in his office and to do what I thought was 'being myself.' Your interactions with your therapist should be your most authentic. If he doesn't know you, he doesn't help you.

Work to expose and challenge important issues. These may be uncomfortable, but if they fester inside you they will be more uncomfortable, more limiting, and more hazardous.

Sometimes painful, this is when the courage comes in. I'm afraid too many don't explore the opportunity therapy presents. Then they feel the 'system' has failed them. Another occasion to make things happen! Go for it.

Digging deep and taking risks in therapy is well worth the effort. When and where the progress shows, however, is another matter. The gain is cumulative, and patience is once again at a premium.

I always look forward to therapy. Many don't. That may not matter; commitment to the process, as well as belief in its capacity, does matter. This is one more base that ought to be touched.

And finally, a good therapist is one who is good for you! If you don't feel you're getting the right attention, the right engagement, appropriate concern and empathy, if the clock gets more eye contact than you... consider a change.

You have work to do. Be stimulating and challenging, making connections from one week to another. There is no progress without you. If your therapist can't command your attention, something is very wrong.

The test is how you are doing. Not always whether you get a big nipple and a fix—although let's not knock these too hard. And of course, we all love to be loved.

I've been favorably impressed by the few therapists

encountered in San Francisco. Unpretentious, honest, committed, Dr. Rischette, when you read this you'll know how grateful I am to you.

Chapter 3
Self-Esteem

Diminished and diminishing self-esteem is cause and effect of depressive illness. It can also be a debilitating part of its legacy. For this reason alone, it is worthy of our focus.

I believe the subject is misunderstood and misrepresented. So are the means for improving it. This is tragic because there is so much that can be done about it.

Put someone in constant psychic pain, add a major stigma, a spiraling confusion, inability to make decisions, inability to cope with life, a feeling of powerlessness and a ravaging despair... and how good can they feel about themselves? Add to this mix a job and career that are failing because of health and a prime relationship that is doomed by inabilities and mood swings, and you have a bio-chemical outbreak.

Everybody who knows you can see that something is

very wrong, but it can't be stated publicly without attracting massive stigma. If you ever *had* self-esteem—and chances are it wasn't solid—you don't now.

Here is what I did to reconstruct self-esteem since May 1994: I withdrew from a relationship before it withdrew from me. My mate of thirteen years (on and off) was worn out by my depressive problems and manic swings. This was understandable; families are decimated by less. She would not recognize me now.

I now felt strong enough to stand up for myself: a triumph on its own. Resolve to act finally led me to seek, find, and sign for a charming apartment two blocks away... in two days. My friend had always said, "when people set their minds to making something happen... it happens." This was the best surge I'd had in years. I was off and running.

Coping well for and by myself was just what the doctor ordered. That this was so visible confirmed the euphoria. The apartment was therapy. I committed myself to it, finding identity and self-possession after disquiet. It was at once outer and inner directed. At last there was a 'me' to come home to.

Other areas came slower. I was no longer working and didn't miss work. Structure has its time and place but I chose to not let it interfere with my lifestyle. I was too vulnerable to my faltering relationship to engage it seriously. This was a weak link, from which I had to move away to survive emotionally. Call this doing what you have to do.

Going to bed late and sleeping later was my habit. Despite society's bias against this, I relaxed into it. We don't have to satisfy all of the mainstream norms at once. My appearance continued to improve, which quickly became a positive esteem issue. I courted MDDA friends like Anne Whitman, who shared my nightmares but understood the urgency to move ahead and had already done so. I will never forget what her friendship meant in the months before and after I moved out on my own— an act unthinkable a year earlier.

The legacy of the past was very much present. I was not noticeably productive, not even busy, but alive and well and stable. That was the good news; the risks were too great not to be cautious. This was a time to avoid failure, frustration and stress. I had enough financial resources to survive, and that relieved what I still felt 'the legacy' would not allow me: managing the pressure, competition, and daily stress of the marketplace. I was committed to not pushing myself against the grain.

The Transcendental Meditation Center in Cambridge, Massachusetts was also a major factor for me from May 1994 on. I spoke at length to Dr. Steele Bullock—a member of the Harvard Medical School faculty who was also TM's medical consultant—about Depression and Meditation. He confirmed my growing sense that Eastern medicine and meditation could be very helpful. (He did say that seriously depressed people should have clearance from their therapists.)

Meditation relaxes the mind and provides a peaceful, calm, spiritual ground, particularly given the nurturing Cambridge association. I started this in an agitated state, and it immediately helped. That I could find an oasis at such a time seemed remarkable. The ideal practice is two twenty-minute, eyes-closed meditations a day. There is also often a group interaction that may add to your comfort and circle of friends. The Tibetan Buddhists meditate with eyes open. I later found this not to my liking.

The Boston TM connection proved more supportive than the San Francisco one, but it came at a more critical time for me. I also tried several sessions of acupuncture in Boston. Many acupuncture professionals specialize in work with depression. This is well worth an open mind. It is ironic that on my trips to medical clinics in China in September 1995, the authorities visited had neither witnessed nor acknowledged depression... Or was this official censorship?

Self-esteem often comes in small, incremental ways. Doing what we want to do, doing what we ought to do, exorcising demons by activities and attitude, accomplishing wherever and whatever we can.

In Fall 1995, I planned and carried out another international trip on my own: Thailand, eight cities in China, Hong Kong. Given my relatively inactive life, it was a bit expansive. But traveling was my love and redeemer. It made me feel proactive, alert and vibrant. It afforded identity.

For much of my life, reacting to uncertainty or adversity, I traveled. It always worked. I read about each country and organized every part of the trip. It was classic empowerment: it made something happen, while satisfying a quest for connection with the planet as well as with all other cultures. A trip to India, Nepal and Tibet in Spring, 2000 brought my total to forty-one countries.

Every reader can find a similar activity and make it happen. Your choices may be simpler, but the key is to make something happen and be proud of it. You are bound to gain confidence. A modest thought, yet a grand experience. Start small, but start.

Others were interested in my trips. I liked that. At the time, I stayed close to those few friends who I loved and trusted. I knew my life was reduced but fought to maintain goals and standards for living. Elusive as it had been, I now pursued comfort as an antidote.

My Boston therapist had said, "Watch your money"—I had overspent in the past, as manic depressives are known to do—"and stay close to your family... Keep your community." I did all of these, shuttling to New York once a month. Personal doubts notwithstanding, I courted stability and spirit. With a quiet resolve, this exercise would pay off in the next few years. These are investments you must make. Forget about going from 'A' to 'Z.'

Appearance

When you don't feel well, dress up a bit," my mother used to say. This is good advice. More recently, a male friend (whose advice I usually ignore) suggested I shave whenever I go out because "you never know who you'll meet." Some depressed (even previously depressed) people look like the wrath of god. If you're suffering, I understand that; if you're feeling a little better, however, tend to your appearance.

Looking better can often make you feel better about yourself. Moreover, it will send a different message to others and they will in turn give you different feedback. Act as if you have self-esteem and it will come to you faster. Like it or not, the world turns around on impressions. Open your options by maximizing your presence.

Handling Your Affairs

In a day to day context, doing the best you can with your personal affairs will make you feel better. If you aren't feeling well, set even a modest standard for functioning and try to sustain it. Do something for your self-interest *and* something you like. Each day, without fanfare, you can make a habit of protecting whatever self-esteem you have. Failure becomes a self-fulfilling prophecy. Limit your responsibilities if necessary but court success on your own terms. Search for pride under every rock and you'll begin to find it. Feeling good about yourself is a habit.

I once wrote what others thought was a brilliant fourteen-page foundation proposal when I was too depressed to do anything else. It surprised even me that out of such torment could come creativity. At a time of despair, I made something happen. Associates regaled me for the writing. It was a miracle—or was it? Find opportunities for positive direction and embrace them. Don't wait for accolades from others. They may or may not come. Give *yourself* license and credit!

Chapter 4

Flow

Can you relax and enjoy while under a depression? Most everyone who has been there knows that you really can't fight depression. You have to give into it somewhat, accept a piece of it while continuing to negotiate in turbulent waters. This is what I call 'flow.' It is tricky.

What can you do despite the depression? It is possible to taste great moments of relief even while the pressure is on. If you can do this, you may well arrest the fear of falling while gaining confidence in your power to withstand. Try to find half an hour a day of 'light.' Then make it an hour, three, four or five. You may amaze yourself. It can be done. And what a triumph! Meditation, I think, is one of those things. Music is another. Conversation with those we trust is another. Surrendering to nature must be another.

Many depressives don't believe they can do what has to be done. How sad! Turn it around and reap the extraordinary benefits. You've left the door open for opportunities that sooner or later will knock. The worst legacy of depressive crisis is the feeling that you can't overcome it. That you are not a survivor. And that the next big wave will roll you around like a twig.

If I had to pick one proud moment in my saga, I think it would be: the affirmation that I will get up if knocked down. Keep an eye on the light at the end of the tunnel, find a way through the moment, find something to accomplish (even if it's washing the dishes), and 'flow' to the brave new day. Finding different ways to experience even modest gains in the middle of depression can resurrect you. Take it seriously, it beats feeling sorry for yourself. This has happened, increasingly, for six years. Do you think I believe it?

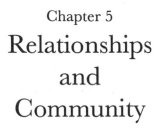

Chapter 5

Relationships and Community

ithdrawal and isolation seem to force themselves on many of us. They are hard to resist when we experience the worst. They serve a purpose when there is nothing else. They don't continue to serve that purpose.

Relationships can be personal or professional. They can be family, friends, same sex, opposite sex, intimate, platonic, emotional, correct, passionate, compassionate. We might reduce the list, but we should do our best with what remains.

Try to be gentle with your family and friends. They will appreciate it and it will nourish you at another level, and perhaps at another time.

In a down period in Boston in the early 90s, I was explosive and sarcastic with my partner. It was an outgrowth of frustration and powerlessness and was a misplaced aggression. Most people exercise their aggressions, day to day, in more functional, socially accepted ways. My therapist told me to stop it. "She will leave you if you don't." I tried never to do it again.

Try not to compare. People are feeling much better than you are, people are succeeding more than you are, people have more than you do. You have a difficult path, because you feel like a loser. It comes with the turf.

You are up against circumstances that others can hardly imagine. Your challenge is to dig in and hold on, while putting one foot in front of the other and trying to inch forward. An enormous task in the grip of serious depression and/or mania. Give yourself some slack. Don't feel bad about feeling bad. You have great courage just to keep going. You are in the fight of your life. Understand that and try to be gentle with yourself. Then find the strength to keep on... because that's what you have to do. If you can integrate all this, it will lighten a heavy burden.

These are tough moments, because you seldom see much light. Own your progress, however small. Work hard to see it, because the illness will deny it. Read the last two sentences again.

At a time when Depression exhausted my ability to concentrate and to get outside myself, I attended a concert and lecture given by the Conductor of the Boston Symphony. To my surprise I noticed that I could listen to and enjoy at least half the program and forget myself. I rejoiced in this because it was the first time in weeks, maybe months, that I could get outside myself.

I thought about it. Sure enough, it marked the start of a much better period. In the worst hours, progress is worth recognizing, acknowledging, and savoring.

Engage people, thoughts and activities unrelated to your illness whenever you can. Any time you can 'lose yourself' in this way, you are building a capability that can serve you.

Also cultivate those who are empathetic, sensitive and compassionate. Those with whom you are comfortable, those who can share your vulnerability. And minimize your contact with those who deflate you (for whatever reason).

Extend your conversation to include the needs and interests of others. This will make you a better listener, better company, and will bring more back to you from other people, allowing you to feel better about your capacities and opportunities. I've had to work hard on this, because it isn't natural to everyone. Try it.

Many years ago, when I was wearing out friends with obsessive, self-centered, repetitive conversation, one of them said to me, quite bluntly, "...you've got to learn how to be with people." He was trying to be there for me, hence I never forgot his comment. The way others perceive you impacts on your identity and self-esteem. Don't throw people away. Make the effort. You have nothing to lose and much to gain.

Chapter 6

Determination and Attitude

"Experience is not what happens to a man. It is what a man does with what's happened to him."
– Aldous Huxley

urmoil and fear plague those seriously depressed, which includes most bipolars at some time. Not only are things bad... they're liable to get worse. Worst of all, we feel no control over what amounts to paralysis. No control, a bitter pill to swallow, weakens resolve.

In more than eight years of attending MDDA (Boston) and DMDA (San Francisco) meetings, I have seen a wide range of determination in members. Granted, it is easier to stand up if we are in reasonable shape; but an unwillingness to settle for a bleak future drives progress. My girlfriend—she much preferred 'significant other'—observed that I was 'stuck.' From that time forward, I tried to be unstuck.

A young woman recently entered my support group pleading for some positive role models. She wanted to hear those doing well or planning to do well. She had lost her income and then her house as the illness carried her to several hospitalizations. Her focus on turning things around was refreshing. I look forward to hearing of her progress. Those who feel better want to leave bad memories behind. The sooner the better.

Group 'business' should be in confidence. Members can be lucid, bright, articulate (about themselves) and open. Though the subject matter is sobering, humor finds its way in. There are many brave souls here, of all ages and backgrounds. Among familiar faces, there are always new faces: in San Francisco, DMDA meets twice weekly, at two sites.

Many in the groups say these are the best moments of their week. Although family visitors may be reserved, members are mostly nourished by interacting and exchanging with those who share their experience. While we don't all speak the same language, we can understand the same language. Vulnerability and authenticity are links.

Attitude is always important. Here it is pivotal because it must compensate for a host of problems. The quality, values and interests you can express will shape your experience. Many don't 'get' this.

If you can work, enjoy art forms, fully participate in conversations on a variety of subjects, act 'normal,' socialize, be interested in food, people, sex... then you are fortunate.

At my worst, I couldn't do any of these. I could talk
to friends on the phone about my issues. That was about
it. How I envied those whose lives had more dimension,
who could easily feign stability and normality. Those suffering cannot pretend very well.

At the Payne Whitney Clinic of New York Hospital,
in early 1981, one of the few recreations I could enjoy
was Scrabble. In succeeding days, after pirating my sev-
enty-nine year old mother from a nursing home to stay
with me at my apartment, I played endless Scrabble
games with her. What a break. She was competitive and
loved to play. This was my life for three months and I
was grateful. Someone who could function at a job had a
big head start. My capacities were limited and I knew it.

Mental issues isolated me at that time, and the state
of the arts in medication was not what it is today. I often
urge group members now to be aware and grateful for
both our Association and the growth and development of
anti-depressants and related drugs.

Chapter 7

Be As Real
As You Can

The thoughts expressed in these pages are not academic. With few exceptions, they weren't read in any book; they come from personal experience.

There must be a connection between sanity, mental health, and the ability to perceive reality, to be real. Yet, reality can be hard to accept. For depressives, it is overwhelming, and it is generally negative. When you don't like the reality, the temptation is to sidestep it, to deny it and replace it with another 'reality,' one more compatible with one's emotional tolerance. People do this all the time. When it becomes continuing habit, however, and where it is an attempt to redirect and rationalize personal feelings, it hinders any progress.

For example, and this is not atypical, I used to get hyper and manic at a time when I thought I was doing well. This often led to a sudden and dangerous fall of spirit and became a pattern. I didn't see the fall coming because I was out of touch with my feelings.

Now I work to stay close to my center and to confront (rather than deny) the reality. This often means giving in. Instead of spiraling, I get productive for a few hours and wait to regain a feeling of control, while accepting uncertainty.

I was real, owned the vulnerability, learned a valuable lesson, and accepted shortcomings. Five years ago I didn't know all this. Do you? It's okay to fail. Just bounce back and remember how you did it.

For those with this illness or predisposition, the knowledge that you can cope and be resilient reduces—if not eliminates—much uncertainty and fear. It can be a self-fulfilling prophecy. "I will not be held hostage by something bio-chemical." (Try telling yourself that).

Set goals you can reach... and reach them. One of my father's sayings was "moderate your desire within the realm of possible achievement." I found that thought too limiting and I resented it at the time. Looking to put one foot in front of the other as we are however, the idea has merit. Repeated failures are debilitating. We need successes to compensate for all that hasn't gone our way. An athletic team builds confidence, in stages, by doing well against opponents of increasing ability. We must prove to ourselves that we can solve problems and move on.

You hear people say, "I'm a survivor." When the illness controlled me, I did not feel like a survivor. If today unnerves you... be good to yourself tomorrow. This can be learned.

Chapter 8

Special Interests

While I don't believe in activity and structure so much for their own sake—others do—inertia and laziness are not luxuries we can afford when under siege. There is something about engaging the mind, the body and the spirit that works! And we must do what works.

It is said there are many bipolar people who are artistic and creative. Historically, renowned political leaders, composers of great music, writers and playwrights have been identified. The list is awesome. It has also been suggested that their disorder 'drove' their creativity. My interests include:

Singing

I have performed popular and jazz classics at celebrated clubs and hotels, mostly in Boston and New York.

I did this part-time over nine years and have been less active the past three years.

I used to regard this as a form of expression and perhaps attention-getting. Several solo performances were successful at moments of severe depression and mania. Stranger still, I had confidence they would work. My life wasn't working but I could pull off the flights of fantasy. On a stage, logic and caution don't carry the day. Before a live audience, I felt that magic blend of inspiration, identity and creation. With ample preparation and attention to detail, I could make things happen on a stage. To do so, however, I still had to believe and be focused.

Today I regard singing as discipline, courage, theatricality, pro-activity, soulfulness. I want mostly to work hard, participate musically, be excellent, be 'authentic,' connect with audiences, be centered musically and personally. If you aren't centered, if there isn't a healthy, declarative 'you' in your performance, then what you do on a stage alienates you further from yourself. We need to reconnect ourselves. Don't allow life to separate you from yourself. If you succeed in promoting a shell of yourself... you 'inherit the wind'.

Appreciate your talents, but cherish most what you can earn and overcome. I take special pride in my comeback.

As a boy, I had decent athletic coordination; but my interest was not in improving and perfecting. It was in looking good. It's fine to want to look good but not if that is all that is happening. I was more concerned about the girls than the game. Focus, hard work and desire surpass talent. Note the great tennis players. And check the level of intensity and excellence in the NBA playoffs.

For me, the winner is the one who values and enjoys the effort. The rest is artifice or self-delusion. To be sure, we can't all have it our way; and we survive as well as we can. But if the choice is ours, let's go for the gold while valuing and enjoying the effort.

One of the many singer-entertainers I admired was Sammy Davis, Jr. I borrowed from the title of his autobiography "Yes I Can" because there are significant parallels.

There was a period in his career when Sammy's performance was falling apart and he couldn't understand why. He taped live shows at the Copacabana in New York and reviewed them repeatedly. The light went on. His act was disintegrating because his personality was fragmenting. he didn't know who he was, was violating himself, and barely had a clue what to do next. When he addressed the root causes, the cloud lifted.

I share this story because all of us have been to frightening places. It is exciting to even imagine that when we gain control of our demons we can find levels of life and expression beyond what we know, that will do us all proud. Call it a leap of faith, but dwell on it a while...

International Travel

International travel may have become a way to compensate for a diminished professional life. I love it and continue to display instincts, resources and energies in traveling creatively on my own. If you like to do something and you develop even a modest history of achieving in it, if you can afford it—do it. Do what gives you pleasure, confidence and pride—particularly if there is something to be learned, and you're not just buying your way.

I study each country's history, character and features and plan the whole trip, avoiding tourists and their patterns whenever possible. One never would have thought I could find my way through 41 countries—satisfying curiosities while pursuing dreams of adventure.

Just a few months ago, however, Tibet proved my undoing. A week of altitudes of up to 13,000 feet, a fever, bad stomach, heatless rooms, doubtful food, uncivilized facilities, and too much bumpy driving through the Himalayas—admittedly breathtaking—combined to derail me. Intravenous feeding was a warning, but none of this rivaled mental illness. I just forgot I'm not Jack Armstrong.

I'd like to believe that travel greatly uplifts consciousness and creates a healthy and expansive universe. Thinking of the cultures I've explored on the world's continents, I am reminded of the delight, accomplishment and freedom I feel in planning and carrying out these trips. But really, anything that engages your mind and imagination is an antidote.

Find something you can be passionate about and get into it. Make it a natural extension of you, your values and energies. You will surprise yourself. It need not be dramatic. It just needs to be you.

A close friend of mine is ushering part time at Symphony Hall in Boston. She loves the concerts, and she makes some spending money. Another friend umpires baseball and softball games. This serves him, it's fun, and he can always do it. Others with an expertise make speeches and are paid, sometimes well. In your heart of hearts, what would you like to try or to do? I wanted to write this book.

Writing

Writing is a vehicle for self-expression, a means to communicate and a way to stimulate and persuade others. I stopped writing for the past four or five years. Why? Because too much of the earlier writing had been to meet the personal priorities and partisan professional agendas of others. With this effort, I return with spirit and stamina.

Do what you can do and do it on behalf of your family, friends and others. Most of all, do it to affirm yourself, your sense of focus, and your desire to emerge from isolation, inertia and fear. That is what all this is about! We ought to dismiss the idea that we're too sick to make a difference in the world around us. That is not helpful.

Your urgency to heal can lift you out of the impasse. Don't make peace with being 'stuck' (as I was called). The more you do—avoiding excessive stress and unnecessary competition—the more you can do, and the less room there is for negativity and self-doubt. Live it and you will know it. But always get the chemical and therapeutic help you need. My message is not about substituting for these.

Comedy

A would-be comic with modest experience is like a retired serial killer. You never know when something might happen. Traditional ethnic humor is self-deprecating. Jews pioneered in this, African-Americans are in it strongly, as are Irish and Italian-Americans. Gays will be in it in the future.

Audiences love comics laughing at themselves. That's why Irish can do drunk stories, Italians can do Mafia stories, and both can do Catholic jokes. I did a decent 'Personals in the 90s' routine, but I might click more on Viagra or age generally. Humor is liberating, stress-reducing, and I think healing—maybe not at the bottom of Depression, but almost any other time.

For example, I like to say "I'm crazy, but I'm not stupid" or "I can accept your craziness but not your stupidity." That's a good one for neurotic types. It defuses 'crazy.' In "Zorba the Greek," Zorba (Anthony Quinn) said, "A man needs a touch of madness." This is therapeutic.

Someday I'll do a manic depressive comedy routine. That would be groundbreaking, although it might take some time for even the mental illness community to loosen up enough to accept it. We're talking about the ability to laugh at yourself. A reflection of health, would you say?

Reading

First, read what you like and value. If you can't read both, read for one or the other. Make the experience a feel-good one.. Otherwise, don't do it. At my worst, I could read only personal growth and/or mental illness revelations. As you feel better, the range of possible reading expands. Almost anything you can do that you value and that gratifies you is progress. There is no such thing as "you are filling your hours and days with more substance and focus and you are still hopeless." I've never heard of that.

Make conscious efforts to improve at least part of your day. We may be stalled in our worst moments; but it can be done. There is something everyone can choose to do at any time—even if that something is sleeping, reflecting, walking, talking. When your health kicks in just a bit, you will experience (or have experienced) a noticeable surge. That's all you need to see some light.

Right now, something bothers me. Yesterday I let myself sleep for more than twelve hours. Today I'll give myself a nice treat and/or delicious dinner. I'll also walk for a few hours. I may call two or three empathetic friends, something I seldom do. And you know what? Today may be on the downside; but tomorrow I'll be back to par.

You may not be able to do this, you may need chemical help, but your day will come. In the meantime, unless you are really immobilized, you can't just sit still waiting for something to happen. You have to pick reachable goals, day to day, however small, and make them happen. To a depressed person, this can sound very difficult, but it can also work. You have everything to gain and almost nothing to lose.

Chapter 9
Friends and Role Models

*"Dignity does not consist in possessing
honors but in deserving them."*
– Aristotle

Depression, frustration, fear and failure attract negativity. These are realities we must acknowledge. So be vigilant and attentive. We have to combat this.

As stated earlier, I spend at least a few hours every week talking and listening to distressed San Franciscans of all ages. They are not melodramatic, not inarticulate, not dull-witted, not weak. They are exhausted by the struggle against manic depression and depression.

For varying reasons, they do not have good support systems. The illness doesn't leave people charming, astute, sensible and resourceful. They are often severely disadvantaged in the give and take of life. I identify with their struggle. Society has finally begun to take mental illness seriously. We must do the same.

A good therapist supports and confronts you, however diplomatically, when necessary. A good friend might do the same. He/she is empathetic, but not twenty-four hours a day. It is better to have some friends, at least, who are not devoured by the illness—who, therefore, have some objectivity, optimism, and good energy to lend. Nobody can be your friend all the time, including your therapist. A handful of people stayed close during my worst hours. I will never forget them.

Someone with serious depressive problems is generally most comfortable talking with those who are similarly demonized. It is that hard for bipolar and unipolar people to feel understood. But you must develop some capacity for disagreeing without being disagreeable, in order to communicate with others. The good news is that developing this capacity will serve you now and in the future.

Do I know how difficult these suggestions are to integrate? I lost a job, a career, a long, valued relationship, pride, hope and confidence. My current outlook is much better than I ever thought it could be, and I protect it fiercely. I also keep the memories and the legacy, because they can serve.

Both my daughters think I am very public about depression. That is part of a continuing crusade to break free, by not running away. Maybe it's also an effort to cut myself some slack, to avoid the stress of having to achieve 'normality' for others.

Affixed to my refrigerator is "Normal People Worry

Me." Dr. Alvin Poussaint, renowned Professor of Psychiatry at Harvard Medical School, said:

> *"... definitions of normal and abnormal behavior are shaped by the values of the society that makes them... The business of what's normal and what's psychopathology gets influenced by culture and politics. It's not hard science."*

Role Models

Role model is a maligned term. People may be models in one segment of our lives and very much not in another. For those of us grappling with unipolar or bipolar illness, a role model can really make a difference—helping us to regain shattered strength and independence while reinforcing the empathy and compassion we've learned.

The examples I hold up have made good efforts to confront past hardship, combine humility with pride, and can relate to those of lesser status or misfortune in a common humanity. On another level, they have self-knowledge, are original, bring a sense of humor to themselves and to life, and have the honesty and courage to stand up for who they are and what they believe.

In the world today, I have most admired Vaclav Havel and certainly Nelson Mandela. Just before them, Dr. Martin Luther King, Jr. For many, if not all of his

*New York Times Jan 15, 2000: "Bigotry as Mental Illness or just Another Norm"

insights and human instincts, I would include President Clinton (now that's courage). Historically, I would also place Paul Robeson high on this list—notwithstanding what I consider his misconceptions about the nature and efficacy of Soviet Russia in his day—for his courageous pursuit of what he felt was just and his exposure of all he felt unjust.

These are choices familiar from public life. From our ranks, I've always admired Anne Whitman of MDDA for her leadership effort in advocacy for issues of mental illness. Anne, who experienced six devastating years herself, made an inspiring comeback—challenging Harvard University for its zeal to 'unload' a woman employee whose manic depressive episodes embarrassed them. Anne helped me to make a critical transition toward independence between 1992 and 1994.

I might add a note of thanks to Wendy Woodfield for her honesty and her persevering effort to expand Boston's Speaker's Bureau. Also Dennis Hagler for his unpretentiousness and thoughtful leadership of the MDDA community of Greater Boston, which he served as President.

Dennis received and responded to my first calls of alarm and agitation in 1992 and from there on, as facilitator of the Massachusetts General Hospital Meeting, was consistently encouraging and inclusive—insuring my stability. He is a man who helps numbers of struggling people without taking credit. He is also someone who came back to serve after a long and disabling personal ordeal.

My values elevate the principles of integrity, honesty, originality, self-knowledge, thoughtfulness, intelligence, liberalism, the capacity to love, and connectedness to the human family. Certainly we can be less lofty. What is important is that our models serve us.

At DMDA, in my year and a half in San Francisco, I salute Claudia Center of the Legal Aid Society for her extraordinary work and commitment to the disabled. Another outstanding leader in the Bay Area is Mark Gottlieb, a former MDDA national president. Mark, an M.I.T. graduate, is one of those people who others always speak of positively. What I admire about both is that they have no personal or hidden agenda, but move effectively to serve and empower the community that so needs their leadership. Fortunately, they seem to get the job done without surrounding themselves with accolades. I might add that SFDMDA has provided much of my introduction to San Francisco—without which the transition from New York and Boston would have been more isolated.

This chapter cannot be closed without a round of applause for the Unitarian Universalist Church (at Franklin and Geary) and St. Francis Memorial Hospital (at Hyde and Pine) for hosting and welcoming our weekly support groups. These are substantial contributions and represent warm, practical acknowledgments that we are here, we seek community, and we are deserving.

Chapter 10
Spirituality, Love, and Generosity

et your quest for deliverance be inclusive. Within common sense, and with the exception of eating, inhaling and drinking things which contradict your prescribed medication, consider alternative approaches.

In my experience, psychiatrists can't do much with seriously depressed patients other than prescribe and hope. However, we still need that presence and support, so I don't suggest we abandon the therapists or the meds. On the other hand, once we pick ourselves off the floor, the doctors tend to know how to consolidate our gains. And they sometimes provide inspired therapy. The question is, can we recognize it?

Spirituality is about things we cannot see, touch or perhaps even explain. If you choose to return to orthodox religious precepts and rituals, if religion meets your needs and gives you peace of mind, comfort and hope, embrace it! Although it doesn't work for me, I believe perhaps it is possible for others. I really rejoice for you.

The rest of us need not forsake spiritual lives because we turn away from traditional religious forms. We have all the more reason to be open. I take it anywhere I find it: Buddhism; Unitarian Universalists; Christianity; Judaism; liberal and humanitarian writings; atheists; agnostics. I read about accomplished, celebrated people: leaders, artists, intellectuals. Can we reconcile what they say with what they do? It's a test that very few pass. You and I have had to look at things squarely. We know the limitations of words.

Listen to poetry, music, a lecture on personal growth, history, art. Spend an afternoon committed to a museum of your choice. Concentrate as well as you can. Can you 'lose yourself' in any part of the experience? If you can, you have gained. This can be learned.

This is not a temporary fix. It is more organic. But you must choose what interests you most. If it doesn't reach you the first time, it might reach the second or third time. I have spent serene moments at the Metropolitan Museum in New York while depressed. This is not a cerebral matter and you needn't believe it to get it. But you ought to try. Our problem is, we often stop trying.

This book is not academic. If something helps you, it helps you. And if it helps you once, it can help you five times. It may be foolish to ignore. In the depths of depression, mood swings were not matters of intellect. Rather, they were about feelings, relationships and connections.

Leave the analysis for afterward, put one foot in front of the other, find the light at the end of the tunnel and focus on it. Your goal is to feel better and better so that you build confidence in your ability to cope and to exercise increasing control.

You don't always have the equilibrium or presence of mind to defend your position to others. Is it really necessary? You are in a battle. Remember the goals. Once you do this, you can revisit the scene. Not before. Protect and correct yourself, but try to resist and reverse whatever makes the struggle seem overwhelming. That sounds like another big task, but it can be done.

Don't try to walk before you crawl. That tires and frustrates. You have little energy to spare. Others have been in your place and done no better. Perhaps they couldn't see any light. If there is ever a time to look into spiritual things, this may be it. And remember your goal: to engage yourself and to feel well enough to keep trying. Remember, just because you can't see the light right now doesn't mean it isn't there. It is.

Love

This will be a stretch for some readers. My mother believed that love heals; I do too. It is redemptive.

Bitterness and negativity are self-destructive when practiced continually. Be positive in your feelings about others as much as possible. If you cannot, control or reduce the interaction. You can surely make that happen. I work at it.

The trick is not to be smiling and positive all the time. That's not real. The challenge is to minimize your contact and conflict with people or activities that seem to violate you—or at least that leave you worse than they find you—and to reach out for what lightens and uplifts. Don't sit and wait for it. Reach out.

I need to heed this. Asserting yourself is one thing. Holding onto things to prove a point when it need not be proved is another. Letting things go, forgetting them if you can't change them, makes sense.

During my ill periods, I felt alienated from much of my environment and wasn't clear why. Vision and judgment were absent. I was repetitive and clueless. It was the best I thought I could do. To find love we have to come from love, and to experience it ourselves. Raw need is not a great start.

I often have to think twice about how to respond to impulse and ego. It gives me relief to embarrass people who I feel treat me unfairly (and I do it with authority). but shortcomings of others can be ignored, particularly with the self-assurance that comes from addressing your own problems directly and forcefully! It is amazing how few of us do that. Bobby Kennedy was known to have said, "I never get in a fight I can't win." Conflict should have a purpose. Misplacing aggressions should not become a habit. Fight for real issues, and for yourself.

People in authority—perceived to have strong egos—seem to manage criticism well. They either diffuse it or defer it until a time they can manipulate it (or you). But that is about power. We're not talking about this kind of power.

What we're talking about is personal empowerment and developing the ability to combat both forms of depression. About actually reflecting love, as opposed to: talking about it; acting as if we don't need answers; placating everybody; being sweet and syrupy all the time; never confronting or getting passionate about anything; never taking positions. These come out of weakness and lack of resolve.

You can have respect and concern for others without losing the courage of your convictions. Find subjects or people who can be the objects of your attention if not affection. Find elements that move and please you... and embrace them. Don't fight windmills.

Many of the mentally ill have dramatic grievances against public figures and institutions. It can become clear that they are externalizing their own frustrations and inertia. There is a strong temptation to do this. It is much harder to look inside yourself for the answers or at least for the problem. Love will give you the energy, and maybe even lead the way. This may sound ethereal, but just try it.

The grievances may be justified. They may even be admirable, but are they taking you where you want to go? Make something happen for yourself. Then wave a flag and we'll pay attention.

A final sobering insight: on some level, in the center of the storm we've been in, we think that we've lost love and affection from others. If we haven't actually lost it, it still feels that way in our isolation. What we might want to do, therefore, is not forego or deny love but revisit it and shape it to our legitimate needs.

Generosity

This can be said in many ways. Let's be simple. It is a quality of heart and soul that allows us to give without receiving. Perhaps it is an act of faith in other people. It can't be missed or denied.

It means sharing. I have made a point of practicing it whenever I can. It is an expression of love that I find life-affirming, particularly when extended without immediate self-interest.

Chapter 11

Decision Making
and Judgement

Depression and mania erode these abilities. At a time when we may need them most, our access is dulled. Among the men and women at MDDA and DMDA meetings I've attended in Boston and San Francisco over eight years, this was more of an issue than people understood.

The reasons are multiple. Sometimes bipolar people don't feel well enough to make decisions and judgments. Sometimes they are so frustrated and unhappy that they can't defer gratification or comfort. They go with the moment, even though it may violate good sense. Either way, they pay a price.

Spontaneity and impulse can be the spice of life, but not in this struggle. If you can find the endurance and the insight to continue thinking ahead, make full use of it. Structure can be your friend.

At the same time, don't get stuck. We look to consistency as an antidote to pain, fear and uncertainty; but it's important to strike a balance that will work for you. As tough as it is, our circumstance calls on us to be adaptive and not always reactive.

Check your decisions and judgments with others. Be a good listener; and don't hesitate to change your mind if all the opinions seem to contradict yours. Your mission is to do what is best for you and to feel better. If you feel better, it may be easier to do what's best for you. Which comes first?

If you must, limit your decisions and weigh your judgments carefully. Take pride in doing your best until the process is more comfortable to you. Remember, indecision and faulty judgment are effects of mental illness, not a cause of it. When we feel better, our faculties will be sharper. Of course, the cause may be partly our medication.

Three years ago, when several of my best friends told me I was overmedicated, I resisted—even feared—the subject. I suppose I thought it was my fate. Dr. Dessain then fine-tuned my prior dosages and added a European drug for mental acuity. To even my surprise, it all worked.

Dr. Rischette continues to adjust my dosages based on my progress. Nothing gives me more satisfaction today than the clarity and flexibility of my mind. At least when I reach for it, it's there!

Chapter 12
Money

As stated earlier, my therapist in Boston cautioned me to watch my money, which bipolar types are notorious for not doing. I was violating this ordinance, part of the self-destructive or at least self-fulfilling prophecy of failure.

Today I watch money closely, making progress in investing while enjoying all opportunities to save. I still spend too freely, but at least it seems under control. This is not only empowering, it colors my financial future and that of my family. It's a great feeling. A blend of coping, self-esteem, prudence, competence, responsibility, and reality. When called 'self-reliant' recently, I valued the compliment. Although I still don't entirely believe it, I'm working on it!

Money is one of many factors in self-reliance; but it is one worth looking at. It is hard enough for us to break through a fragmented past. A sensible relationship to money is a big step forward. It serves both financially and psychologically. I can't always remember which issue came first. I remember well, however, that by early 1994 I was on a collision course with my resources and caught it just in time. When my very practical girlfriend started drafting budgets for me, I knew my time was up. There are times to spend and times not to spend. Be clear on the difference.

Chapter 13

See the Connection Between What You Do and How You Feel

"Without a measureless and perpetual uncertainty, the drama in human life would be destroyed."
– Winston Churchill

Nuts and bolts issues for all of us, while in the heat of the struggle, are too often overlooked. There are activities and individuals, however few, which we can tolerate even under duress and which may even interrupt the melancholy. Talking on the phone to friends, walking, reading, philosophy, psychology and music are familiar examples. Whatever most relaxes you.

I could also write and sing effectively. What came from the heart, from emotions, feelings, relationships, sometimes instincts... could provide moments of direction. What was cerebral, outer-directed, ego-oriented, competitive, strong-willed was generally neither useful nor functional.

For the better part of two years in 1992 and 1993, I was job hunting while depressed, a disastrous experience.

There were more than two hundred targeted individual letters, some seventy personal interviews (including second and third visits), all at quality level. I came in second and third many times, but never first. This included a dozen expenses-paid trips to other cities. I was too depressed to be doing this, and it had to be obvious. My work called on me for resilience, personality, animation and leadership. I was driving on empty.

A therapist confided that I was digging a track in the brain with this activity. At the same time, my mate was urging me on, losing confidence daily in her non-achieving guy. I needed someplace to hide. It was a bad time.

Since then, I've come to see that I never really liked my work, which was related more to meeting other people's needs than my own... particularly others with money and power.

It was the wrong thing at the wrong time. I wouldn't do this work today, notwithstanding the extraordinary institutional affiliations it provided, including a number of the country's cultural icons. Finally, none of it could relieve depression and manic depression. Can other things? I believe so.

Today I know instantly—well almost instantly—what I feel about people and circumstances. I know that my travel is adventurous, colorful, proactive and liberating. Also that it is admired and respected by most people. I feel able to plan and organize trips creatively, while using my travel experience to save money. Forty-one countries already visited include all of Western Europe, Central Europe, Northern Europe and most of Eastern Europe; almost all of Asia (including Japan and China); Australia and New Zealand; the former Soviet Union, and others.

I often planned trips right after depressive episodes and felt exhilarated. These were declarations of renewal after months of loss. They made me feel good about myself and the future. If the acknowledgment isn't given to you, take it.

This may not be everyone's style. There are endless avenues open to you, perhaps less dramatic but equally nourishing, that may not be accessible to me. Whoever thought I would really write this book?

There are always ups and downs in life. Nobody reaches all the goals. Nobody avoids all the frustration. The average person has every day to get up and make something happen. At the least, we all want to feel we're in the ball game and we have some control over the elements of winning and losing.

Tune in to what serves you. And, if you can, quit what doesn't serve you. Don't keep doing what doesn't feel good unless you have to do it. Even then, question it. This alone will bring rewards you can't see. Many have no idea what really serves them. We can't afford that.

Chapter 14

Patience

"Courage is resistance to fear, not absence of fear"
– Mark Twain

r. Tom Perls, Chief of Gerontology at Harvard Medical School, heads the New England Centarian Project, studying 169 people who have lived more than a century. Among other things, he learned that they share certain personality traits:

> *"They tend to be unfailingly optimistic about life; they score very low—which is very good—on the neuroticism scale; and they love to laugh and do so often... There is no substitute for looking at life and seeing the glass 'half full' rather than 'half empty.'"*

Neuroticism, Dr. Perl explains, is the inability to let go of the kind of negative things that happen to all of us. He says those who dwell on setbacks have a hard time dealing with the changes that commonly accompany advancing age. "It's all a matter of how you handle it," he says.

There's a lesson here for all of us. Even with our imposed exile and the neuroses, we can all do better in minimizing the damage. We can try to practice humor, patience and optimism. We can at least make a dent in each of these. Progress is cumulative!

Patience is a tough one. We have to work hard on it. But what we can do is measure gains, incrementally, to recognize and value each sign of growth and resiliency. Trust me.

Every early recovery from a setback or disappointment is a victory over our past (whereas others take it for granted). For these reasons, I see patience as the spirit and resolve to accept progress on its own timetable, while laying the groundwork for a healthier future.

Typically, many people feel they are not up to patience in the face of such stress and distress. Be impatient about your progress and your health only where it serves you, just as I am impatient about getting this book right.

There is a light at the end of the tunnel somewhere that summons you (or your loved one). Keep your eye on that light. We 'own' what we earn and achieve... what we make happen. And yes, it is empowering.

In July of 1998, owners of my three family building in the South End of Boston passed a letter under my door, indicating their intention to convert to a single residency. I had six weeks to find a new home and leave.

The apartment was my refuge and my stability. For what seemed less than a minute, I was distraught, suspecting that I couldn't replace it at anywhere near the rent, and feeling disinclined to try.

Then I thought, "I'll move to San Francisco!" where my brother and his family and my older daughter have lived for many years. More than a dozen visits to the Bay Area over some thirty years had persuaded me, several times, that it was a nirvana and that I ought to be there.

At an MDDA meeting an hour later, fortunately, I shared the letter and my new resolve. Friends claimed to be saddened but impressed by my recuperative power and balance.

Several weeks later I flew to San Francisco and, with the help of my brother, found a terrific apartment in three days, paid three months rent, and prepared to set off for a long-planned month in Asia. I packed and shipped the Boston apartment, went to Vietnam, Japan, South Korea, Taiwan and Hong Kong, and returned to live in San Francisco in October of '98.

I had never responded to serious reversal with such clarity and focus. It was also the best way to move through a potentially destabilizing challenge. Who knows where the inspiration began or ended? It was a milestone I would not have believed could happen.

I never looked back and never regretted the decision. It felt dangerously normal. This was not like me. My brother and daughter have been helpful on the west coast, and I reached out early to San Francisco DMDA.

I keep in close contact with selected Boston friends and with the two doctors there responsible for my health and improved outlook. Of course, my younger daughter and her mother in New York, and my other New York friends remain priorities.

Guess what? Everything is not perfect here. My social life is not exactly happening and I miss family and good friends from the east, but my medical network is in place and all else is progressing. I have planned and completed another trip abroad; started to sing a bit with one of the Bay Area's stellar jazz pianists; joined the Commonwealth Club, World Affairs Council, and Asian Art Museum; assaulted San Francisco's formidable ethnic restaurants; done up an apartment; and explored the Bay Area's diversity and charm on foot.

It is less than two years later and despite shortcomings, life is improving more often than not. What more can one want than a 'shot at the gold'? Younger I can't be. But if health, the stock market and a passion for life hold up, I'm still happily chasing my rainbow and the fairy princess.

In the mid-late 1980s, I worked with Cliff Helman in a Black-Jewish alliance in Boston for the flagship social service agency, Lena Park Community Development Corporation. I admired Cliff, then in his 60s and a former president of Combined Jewish Philanthropies. During a lengthy conversation, he revealed that he had played halfback some forty years earlier on a pretty good Harvard football team. As the kind of would-be jock most men are, I couldn't resist engaging the subject. "You must have been good, because you aren't that big." "I was fast," he barked. "With a good block and one step on the defender, I was gone." This meant, with a good start and any daylight between me and the goal line, nobody could catch me from behind. I never forgot this image.

You can't score a touchdown lying down; you need to be in physical motion to gain sufficient momentum. You have to believe in yourself and your ability. You need courage, a second effort, the right instincts, a commitment to excel, hard work and discipline... and maybe a little luck.

Keep your eyes on the goal, be as active as you can, be poised to break away from the memories that plague you. Never stop believing that you can rise to the occasion. And find what you have long wanted by gaining ground, however slowly.

Chapter 15

Disappointments
and Reversals

*"Experience, which destroys innocence,
also leads people back to it."*
– James Baldwin

Failure, or more particularly, blows to the ego, can be devastating to the biochemically vulnerable. This can relate directly to professional and personal rejections. Unfortunately, it can also apply to those many instances where we perceive almost every action or interaction as a disappointment or reversal.

This is a problem, because without a healthy ego, without some self-esteem, it is treacherous to navigate and keep your balance in the mainstream. The negative perceptions go along with this.

Let's look at it. In a healthy relationship, there is always a give and take. People are too busy, too stressed themselves, to constantly be tender, supportive, forgiving, deferential—unless they are 24-hour-a-day caretakers, so vulnerable themselves that they walk on eggshells and avoid confrontations, even with a spouse or partner.

Almost by definition, there is a need for each partner to carry his or her own weight; to be strong and balanced enough—in short, healthy enough—not to pull the other down!

When the illness dominates, most of us have trouble not only behaving normally, but also perceiving normally. Too often our social abilities and objectivity are impaired, our corrective mechanisms faulty. This makes partnerships or interactions perilous. Generally we know this; and we are sensitive, perhaps pained by it.

Acknowledging and accepting reality assumes a bit of strength that most people take for granted. Too often, depressives lack the clarity and psychological balance to compete, to take the blows, to neutralize life's stresses. For this we pay a big price; because, sooner or later, life is demanding for everyone.

It works for me to 'own' disappointments and reversals. Not too long ago, I traveled to India, Nepal and Tibet. My older daughter, knowledgeable about travel and certain of herself, said, "Why are you going to Tibet? What do you expect to find there?"

She was right. I was over my head for the first time traveling. The other half of my tour group—the first I've chosen in five years—and I were joined by fourteen strangers for the drive from Kathmandu, Nepal on into Tibet, through the Himalayas for four days and finally to Lhasa, the central city of Tibet. Our group included two young men from France, a Korean, Italian, two

Canadians, a sardonic Brit, a confident married couple from Colorado, an acerbic young woman from Ohio, and my original English-American tour partner.

They were all about the age of my daughters (in their early thirties). Rounding out the group were a pleasant Irish woman (living in London) closer to my age, and a robust Norwegian couple of 67 and 73 who had three grown and accomplished children and who had been trekking, camping and skiing in cold climates all their lives. Leading the group was a Tibetan guide, a kind and warm man of 35 or 40, without whom the story that follows would be considerably worse.

A harbinger of troubles to come was the group of ominous Chinese officials at the border: our van quickly stalled in the mud on deficient roads, and the first of many uncivilized bathrooms appeared. Add on: a high fever (for a day or more), standard bad stomach, basic accommodations that, with one or two exceptions, redefined my sense of 'basic,' six to seven hours a day of driving on bumpy roads, minimalist food, interminable begging, and worst of all, hotels devoid of physical warmth.

I was sick throughout the week, at one time needing intravenous feeding. And not a single depressive to share it with—instead, wall to wall normal people. It took ten more days including five in New York, to feel better. I lost ten or fifteen pounds and much confidence. The trip, despite good days in India and Nepal, was a disappointment and, in another sense, a reversal. I wasn't rugged enough. And my judgment was faulty in the first place.

Throughout earlier bipolar days, I coveted the smallest successes. Failures had taken their toll. Moderated goals and safeguards limited my stress. In Tibet, however, I couldn't cut my losses. There were no planes, trains or greyhound buses leaving the Himalayas. I had to 'do the time' until we got to Lhasa, and even there I barely got up for meals.

Everybody else, it seemed, went along with the program. They appeared energized, though perhaps they weren't. As my therapist later pointed out, the vulnerability was damaging to someone with my harsh memories of being defenseless. Things were out of my control. I couldn't stop the world and get off. Not nearly as bad as depression, to be sure, but connected by association of symptoms. Actually, I thought I took it rather well.

Upon my return, I told Dr. Rischette that I didn't think I was depressed and wasn't fearing depression, "but I am way down." He nodded. The Tibet experience had defeated the purpose of traveling, or so it felt.

At this point, I went to work: accepting disappointment and neutralizing reversal. I made phone calls to friends, sang a bit with my tapes, organized my trip pictures, re-ignited my love affair with San Francisco, coaxed a rise in the stock market, took steps to juice up my social life, and returned to writing my book! I started to make things happen and to feel better about myself, my power, my control. It worked.

If we can come to see disappointments and reversals
as opportunities to affirm our resilience and endurance,
we gain. If we can abide our fears, we are coping with
life—experiencing setbacks as mere impediments on a
steep climb. We can then act on our own behalf. That is
a reassuring trumpet. We will always face disappointment and reversal. Everyone does.

Each time I fall, I seem to get up just a bit faster. I
savor that. Be your own best friend. Set modest goals
every day: get up earlier, get more sleep, walk a mile on a
nice day, converse with a pleasant stranger, make someone happy, seek out someone you like, find a few reasons
to like yourself, start something and finish it, smile so
that tomorrow you may even laugh, act as if you feel
good! Here is where you need a touch of trust. As trivial
as these may sound, they work. See for yourself.

Circumstances need not be dramatic to be real and
gainful for you. Seize your moments. Nothing succeeds
like success. *Redefine success in your own terms.* I continue to
do things that were out of my grasp a short while ago; I
just don't push the envelope too far or too fast. That
would be counter-productive and, in fact, I've seen it end
disastrously for others in manic stages.

Chapter 16
Stigma

ven the suggestion of mental illness troubles many otherwise thoughtful people. It was true in my parents' day and although the climate has greatly improved, the subject confounds many today. We can tell by the facial expressions, and by the inane questions asked.

We already see the statistics. Only one out of three who need medication and therapy take it; and our members continue to fight the health care establishment for some parity with other illnesses. I have seen friends and family avoid the very medical circumspection they would covet were the diagnosis cancer or heart disease. The cost of this oversight, in the first decades of the 21st century, will be substantial.

There is a cadre of thoughtful, committed folks, including my good friends already mentioned, who fight on to destigmatize all that we are confronting. They are 'advocates,' in the best sense, for the cause. I salute them. They open doors to understanding and reconciliation. That would remove one huge barrier for those who choose to reenter the mainstream to support themselves, their families, and their dreams of wholeness.

My daughters, in different ways mentioned earlier, have commented that I wear bipolar on my sleeve. If it is true—I wasn't thrilled to hear it—here is my response: I fought the fight, paid the dues, saw the light, came out of the tunnel with pride intact and a measure of confidence. Unlike some others, I choose not to forget—and I keep in contact with many others who can't forget. This is not mere generosity; it is also self-interest.

I have now lived long enough and independently enough to withstand and detour many societal roadblocks. So to celebrate my health and to strike a blow for all those who don't have the wherewithal to elevate the struggle... I emerge from anonymity. It feels good. More importantly, I hope it makes a difference.

Chapter 17
Legacy

Perhaps it is prophetic that my former mate from '81-'94 will be married just before this book is published.

The memory of my long relationship, filled with discomfort as well as with many positives, is inseparable from my illness. Fragmented egos can't build creative partnerships—particularly not with strong, decisive, ambitious partners. And though I didn't see it this way until recently, she probably did her best. I'm sorry about all of it. Depression and manic depression make terrible bedfellows.

Similarly, my career waned under the illness. Unlike more recent interests, I lacked the energy and stability to defer so much gratification and to play 'games' others chose... and by their rules. Hopefully, you can stay closer to yourself—thereby at least fighting those battles that really mean something to you.

I don't miss my work. That is barely an issue. I'm more at peace than ever which is, after all, a relative statement.

Four families represented their bipolar loved ones at DMDA meetings earlier this year. Two grandparents on behalf of their grown grandson, a young man concerned about his mother, a 32-year-old woman alarmed about her husband's bizarre (manic) behavior in the past two months, and another young man who wanted to be able to understand what is happening to his wife, who is bipolar.

Their involvement was moving. It was also a sign of enlightened progress. One might hope it was the culmination of all the best advocacy efforts by Anne, Dennis, Wendy and others. Public perception is improving and expanding. And continuing love and support from family and friends is a lifeline for all of us who grapple with mental illness. I'll spare you stories of families dismissing, ignoring and being hostile to our members. This is not only a sad, tragic commentary; it lowers the outlook and opportunities for thousands of people. Frankly, I had no such family experience.

MDDA and DMDA meetings encourage connection and a sense of belonging between members, as well as between members and their families. It is important and therapeutic. Nothing can stop an idea whose time has come. Although not always acknowledged and recognized by the hundreds of people who attend, 'connection' is a lifeline.

Chapter 18

Yesterday, Today and Tomorrow

"I shall tell you a great secret, my friend.
Do not wait for the last judgement.
It takes place every day."
– Albert Camus

Nobody gets what he or she wants all the time. We who talk mostly to others in the movement tend to forget that. What we really want (or should want) is a 'turn at bat'... to come to the plate, to have a chance to compete. What we don't want is to be 'stuck,' to stay in the same place. That is falling behind.

My former partner told me (in 1993) that I was 'stuck'. I hated to hear it. But it was true. We may all be stuck at times, but we can work on that. To be stuck all the time is another matter.

That was yesterday. We can make peace, however uneasy, with the yesterdays in our lives. We can and should learn important lessons from them. We cannot change or reconstruct them. Today is upon us. Hopefully, we can address it authentically. Not only to live fruitfully, but to prove to ourselves that we can renew.

Sometimes dramatically, mostly undramatically, we must confront the todays before they are the yesterdays.

Many of us don't challenge the quality of our days because we can't confront the inertia and vulnerability brought by mental illness. This is understandable. Yesterday wasn't, the day before wasn't, and the day before that wasn't. Why should today be? The answer is we have to find it or create it. A hard answer for those who feel well, a 'mountain' for the rest of us to climb.

Once we make things happen, we can make them happen again. Then the yesterdays—fruitless and joyless—may be subdued. "Easier said than done," you say. Maybe. But don't quit before you start. This is the one step at a time program. We didn't fall down the hill all at once and we won't come back up with a push and a pull. Set yourself daily goals and when you reach them, climb ever so gently the next day. If you must skip a day or two, do so. Then continue.

There were times when none of us looked back. The view was too frightening, too dysfunctional. I choose to remember those times; but only if they can lead, with courage and insight, to Today and Tomorrow.

Are there moments of doubt? Yes. Is the journey without impediment? Is anything worth achieving ever easy? Never. But it can get easier with self-assurance and a track record of taking control of whatever is important to our lives. For everyone who can't do that, there are three or four who can but think they can't.

Are there issues, circumstances, moods that threaten to derail us? Yes. How do we handle them? We push most when we feel the strongest and clearest, and with guidance from a good therapist and the appropriate medication. Trusting ourselves is difficult given our history. But we must make it happen.

I tell myself: "If you write a book like this, you have to live it. If you talk the talk, you'd better walk the walk. Otherwise, no one will read your book and take you seriously." That threatens me and I get on with it!

Earlier this year I visited with a group member who had delivered herself to a hospital, hopefully for a short stay. She shared with me thoughts about suicide, about her sister and mother, about childhood, emotional abuse. I was shaken by this and hadn't realized it. She had seemed less complex than her history. Mea culpa.

A male friend in the group confided that his parents, particularly his father, never could accept him as gay. Next, they couldn't accept his depression—institutionalizing him for long periods when he returned from years away and sought to communicate and be understood.

A third group member revealed that his stepfather used to beat his mother and him when he was eight or so. His stronger memory was hiding behind his mother while his stepfather was hitting her!

My past seems sheltered next to these. Am I an intruder, an impostor? Their backgrounds deserve more time, work and understanding. Yet it is for these friends I also write and to them I speak. They are deep in my thoughts. (If I prayed, they would be in my prayers). These people must open this up as well as they can. Their issues demand it.

In March 1999, in the British West Indies, I took one of my many lithium-related bad physical falls. Lithium, which I've used for 19 years, is known to effect a part of the brain that controls balance. The fall immobilized my right shoulder for several weeks. I worked out of this gradually with reduced exercises. Yes, the physical issues are easier than the psychological. But let's try to be patient with depression until we see progress.

'Tomorrow' appears in many shapes and forms in America's culture and literature. "The sun will come out tomorrow" is the opening line of the song "Tomorrow" from the celebrated early 80's musical "Annie." My younger daughter, Lilia, loved the song and I'd like to think she also loved the message of resurgence and resilience. She sang it at a showcase with entertainer friends. John Shuck, who played Daddy Warbucks in "Annie" on Broadway, joined Lilia at our table. "Tomorrow, tomorrow, I'll love you tomorrow... Tomorrow's another day." That photo on the kitchen wall still talks to me.

So many popular songs have been about tomorrow. So many books have 'tomorrow' in the title. Tomorrow is the future, the unknown, the unfolding, the place where plans and expectations can come together and bear fruit.

Lyrically, it is the home for our dreams. We didn't do it yesterday, we won't do it today, but on some tomorrow...

Arizona Senator and recent Presidential candidate John McCain was beaten and tortured for five years as a prisoner of war in Vietnam. It was then that he dreamed of being a future United States president. For all we know, it kept him alive. Such is the power of hopes and dreams for the future. John McCain was neither unipolar nor bipolar, although at times, as a prisoner, he must have been a reasonable facsimile. But were he really one of us, he would not have lasted long in that circumstance.

Almost by definition, those most plagued by this illness are sobered, if not paralyzed, by their future prospects and opportunities. After all, if their past and present experiences are lacking, how confident can they feel about the future? That prospect bodes ill for the many tomorrows.

The father of Leonard Bernstein—the late and celebrated composer, conductor and prolific musical personality—felt that at seventy, he would be at the peak of his decline and life would then be downhill. In fact, he died at seventy-one.

Leonard Bernstein repeated the pattern. Possessed by this demon, he also went quickly downhill emotionally and physically, and died just past seventy. Both of their glasses were 'half empty.' They had lived youthful, active lives and couldn't make the transition to seventy. I understand age phobia, but they simply gave up and gave in to their worst fears. Self-fulfilling prophecy.

This we cannot afford. And here is what I would do about an outlook toward the future:

• **Invest in areas of interest.** Find activities and affiliations that you enjoy and that engage you, even if for limited time periods. Remember, the more you can do this, the more capacity you develop. Ability to focus is critical to performance, to cognitive ability, and to state of mind.

Isolation tends to reinforce depression. Get out of yourself; it will pay dividends. I attend lectures and forums of substance on subjects of interest, including such diverse areas as personal growth and international relations. Museums may do more for you than you expected. But you must make choices and commit your attention. Consult your newspaper for local events, exhibitions, and street fairs (I love fairs, city and country). If money is an issue, pick free events. If you can expand your comfort and interest zone, you are doing something important for yourself. This may sound hard to do. But guess what? Many of you never tried it. I know it is impossible in your lower depths, but when you feel better, that's the time to start.

• **Extend yourself to family and friends**. The litany of failed and failing family relationships in DMDA and MDDA is alarming. It is also understandable. Good relationships take energy, life-force, generosity of spirit, and forgiveness. Those to and for whom I write do not feel they have these to give. I see the problem.

Dr. MacMillan in Boston encouraged me to stay close to my family. That was that. As indicated earlier, I wouldn't have a story to tell were it not for my daughters and their mother. Since coming to California, I have reunited with my brother and his family, and with my older daughter and her family. Admittedly, my mother, who I think was undiagnosed bipolar, had trouble accepting my illness, but she was as supportive as her advanced age would allow.

The illness disconnects you. You have to work harder to connect. Whether family or friends, it will come back to you. The key is 'giving.' People turn off to you because you don't participate or return what they give. You can reach out at almost any time and doing so will help you. I believe I have good relationships with family and friends because I always try to give to them. That's a priority. Everyone wants love and attention. Make it a priority. Extend yourself and see what comes back to you. It is a natural law that has changed my life. It came hard at first and has gotten easier.

• **Exercise regularly**. Swimming, walking, calisthenics, even housecleaning, give me a feeling of mobility, discipline, self-control and accomplishment. What starts as a labor can become a pleasure. Fortunately, I like exercising. Jogging sustained my interest for many years, but swimming is better and healthier. Pick something you like and apply yourself. Don't expect to like it immediately. When I moved to San Francisco, I made it a priority to live within walking distance of my favorite pool. I'll never be an Olympian but I swim two or three times a week (eighteen one-way laps) and covet the reward. Doctors suggest that appropriate exercise increases endorphins in the body. This is known to elevate mood. I can't remember a time when exercising did not lift my mood, however briefly.

• **Meet new people**. Whether you're eager to do so or not. If you can do it, you'll be surprised. Talk with them. Find common ground. This will get easier. I regard socializing as an acquired habit.

• **Keep abreast of local, national, international issues**. Read the paper. If you can't, read the summary. Find something in it that commands your attention. I know there is a connection between interest in issues and ability to function. If you must obsess, find some new subjects!

• **Do what feels good to you**. But start expanding now. There is also a correlation between what interests you and your capacity to grow. Reach for what can engage you and pursue it. Something feels good to you;

follow it.

Collectively, these all extend your range of opportunity to get out of yourself and to participate. They will build confidence in your own judgment, capacity and stability. This is invaluable. What may start as a burden can suddenly become a lifestyle.

I've pushed myself toward people and activities, often with surprising rewards. The key is to do what feels right for you and what works, not just to be busy. Be aware of how you feel, and let your actions follow suit. I had to learn this the hard way, because I was in the habit of ignoring vital signs. If it turns you off, you'll want to know. Nothing ventured, nothing gained.

Make your tomorrow. It is possible and what a sense of satisfaction. I am not always happy. Nobody is. But I try not to stay in the same place two days in a row, not reaching for home runs, but always making contact with the ball. This baseball reference means, put one foot in front of the other and accept incremental progress.

Be kind to yourself. When you get a real compliment, understand it and cherish it. Learn to be proud of yourself. I do some dumb things; and I think, what a dumb thing to do or way to behave. Recently, I had what seemed at first a manic outburst—in front of an audience yet. I forced myself to learn from it and move past it. There's no need to deny things like this. There's also no need to go on about how absurd you were. The healthiest people make fools of themselves, many of them in public office. What's important is letting go and moving on. If you're going to dwell on something, make it success.

Wherever you are, you can move forward. You may not recognize the changes, but they will be real and enduring, and they will energize you in ways beyond your imagination. After a fairly slow period, my life is starting to snap, crackle and pop. It had to: how could I end this book on a down note? After all, bad news you don't need.

Be vigilant. Today comes and goes. But as the James Bond movie proclaimed, "Tomorrow Is Forever."

Conclusion

'**ve** said that my daughters, both strongly supportive of this book, have questioned my increasing openness about what has always been a taboo and a stigma. I outlined my response to them at a February, 2000 DMDA meeting:

My progress has come not at once but over many years. I am proud to have held my own against a Goliath—a demoralizing, debilitating, isolating, shame-provoking, terrifying emotional and physical experience.

I see too many others frustrated, exhausted, and immobilized by both forms of depression. A large number are men and women of all ages who lack the family support, personal resources, and, due to years of negative experience, self-esteem and energy—not the brains—to stand up for themselves. Part of their deficit has to be the legacy and stigma of mental illness.

The advantages of much improved health, morale, and lifestyle inspire me to share what I have learned and experienced with those who most need support. These are people, often of high character, substance and intelligence, who are paying a high price with unipolar and bipolar depression. It is for them and to them that I write this book with the hope and dream that it will add to their lives as it is adding to mine.

There was once a fervent and humble preacher in a small Baptist church in North Carolina who addressed this message to his congregation: "We're not what we wanna be. We're not what we oughta be. We're not what we gonna be. But Lord, we ain't what we was!"

To all of you in the struggle, and to your friends and families, keep on keepin' on. You have a brighter future than you can imagine. I know you, hear you, am one of you...

"Yes You Can!"

Biographical Note

Richard Aaron Mead was born at New York Hospital long ago, the son of professional parents who lived in Manhattan, the Bronx and Queens. He and his older brother were products of the New York Public School system.

He was a popular leader at Forest Hills High School, but in his first month at Hamilton College, an academic enclave in upstate New York, his world fell apart. Experiencing the first of his recognizable depressive episodes—not very well understood by anyone in those days—both derailed his first year and set a vulnerable tone for the years ahead. He somehow graduated with a degree in English Literature (and a reputation as a romantic actor).

Shortly thereafter, he adopted Greenwich Village in New York, married, and began to raise two daughters.

'The Village' became at once his refuge and his identity.

In 1967, he earned an M.A. in Political Science and International Relations at New York University in Washington Square—a short walk from his home. It sounded progressive, but underneath there was well-defended turbulence, covered by personality, talent and physical health.

It wasn't until January 1981 that he was diagnosed as bipolar and entered Payne Whitney Clinic (New York Hospital), whose depression study unit was a national pacesetter. Four difficult months after leaving the hospital, he was stabilized on Lithium and another drug, and promptly travelled abroad, a pattern he followed for years. Despite New York's distractions, only his family, good friends and creative instincts remained 'center and sanctuary.'

In 1992, he joined weekly MDDA (Manic Depressive and Depressive Association) meetings at Massachusetts General Hospital in Boston, where he then lived. Many of his best friends came from this group, which he credits strongly. He was moved by the support here, none of which he could find in New York eleven years earlier.

With MDDA as a resource and forum, in May 1994 he started meditating and switched to Prozac in the same week. His improvement was almost immediate and marked a new stability and climb toward greater health and expression. Continuing medicating, including Lithium and Prozac, he has had no further episodes to

the present day. As he is quick to indicate, however, he is
cautious, conscious and dedicated to maintaining mental
health.

In October 1998 he moved from Boston to San
Francisco, where he immediately connected with DMDA
at Saturday afternoon and Monday evening meetings.
He credits San Francisco's affiliate of Boston's MDDA as
the prime factor in this transition and continues to share
weekly in its activities.

His work in 'institutional development' over many
years included the New York Public Library (and its
Library for the Performing Arts), The American
Shakespeare Theatre, and Carnegie Hall. During this
time he conceived and produced campaigns and gala
evenings with celebrated classical, popular, and jazz
artists.

The author is proudest of his warm association and
history with two grown daughters who are flourishing:
Lilia, as owner and director of *"Go Yoga"* in Williamsburg,
Brooklyn, one of the newest and most successful centers in
New York; and Darya, an accomplished writer-producer
at a San Francisco television production company. Their
mother, Cynthia, who has a dedicated career working
with women at the New York City Department of Health,
shares their commitment to this book.